Discover India
State by State

# OFF TO
# HIMACHAL PRADESH

## SONIA MEHTA

PUFFIN BOOKS

An imprint of Penguin Random House

PUFFIN BOOKS

USA | Canada | UK | Ireland | Australia | New Zealand | India | South Africa | China | Singapore

Puffin Books is part of the Penguin Random House group of companies whose addresses can be found at global.penguinrandomhouse.com

Published by Penguin Random House India Pvt. Ltd
4th Floor, Capital Tower 1, MG Road,
Gurugram 122 002, Haryana, India

Penguin
Random House
India

First published in Puffin Books by Penguin Random House India 2017

Picture Credits
P 13: Dalhousie, Himachal Pradesh (mdsharma/Shutterstock.com); P 20: Himachali house (volobotti/Shutterstock.com); P 22: Elderly Himachali couple (Erofeenkov/Shutterstock.com); P 23: Kullu Dussehra procession (© Kondephy (Own work) [CC BY-SA 3.0 (http://creativecommons.org/licenses/by-sa/3.0)], via Wikimedia Commons); P 24: Phulech Fair (Murgermari/Shutterstock.com), Losar Fair (Zzvet/Shutterstock.com); P 29: Chintpurni Fair (© Gopal Aggarwal from India [CC BY 2.0 (http://creativecommons.org/licenses/by/2.0)], via Wikimedia Commons); P 30: Traditional Himalayan house (volobotti/Shutterstock.com); P 32: A colonial cottage in snow (Niranjan Gaikwad/Shutterstock.com); P 42: A woman weaver (Murgermari/Shutterstock.com); P 44: Road side food stall (Murgermari/Shutterstock.com); P 48: Himachali house (Vadim Petrakov/Shutterstock.com); P 49: Mother and child wearing traditional Himachali clothes (diybe /Shutterstock.com)

The views and opinions expressed in this book are the author's own and the facts are as reported by her, which have been verified to the extent possible, and the publishers are not in any way liable for the same.

The information in this book is based on research from bona fide sites and published books and is true to the best of the author's knowledge at the time of going to print. The author is not responsible for any further changes or developments occurring post the publication of this book. This series is not a comprehensive representation of the states of India but is intended to give children a flavour of the lifestyles and cultures of different states. All illustrations are artistic representations only.

ISBN 9780143440826

Design and layout by Quadrum Solutions Pvt. Ltd
Printed at Repro India Limited

www.penguin.co.in

This is a legitimate digitally printed version of the book and therefore might not have certain extra finishing on the cover.

# Hello Kids!

I'm so happy you are reading this book. India is an incredible country and there are lots of things about it that we never get to hear about.

I discovered India because my father was in the Indian army. He was posted to many places all over India—and we dutifully followed him. Can you imagine that by the time I was in the tenth standard, I had changed nine schools? Of course it was hard making new friends almost every year, but the good part was that I got to live in so many places. Right from Kerala, where I was born, to Kashmir, Jhansi, Shillong, Chandigarh, Goa . . . the list is long.

Every time I go to a new place, I feel amazed at how different each state is from the other—and yet, how similar. Did you know that we can see monuments from the Stone Age right here in India? Or that we have more than twenty official languages, and most Indians know three or four on an average? Or even that some of the world's most amazing scientific marvels were invented in India?

Oh, there are many, many, many fun and fantastic things about the states of India, which we simply must get to know.

So get your backpack ready, get set to meet some new friends and join me on a fun trip as we DISCOVER INDIA, STATE BY STATE.

I hope you enjoy reading this book as much as I have enjoyed writing it. I would love to hear from you. So do write to me at sonia.mehta@quadrumltd.com.

Lots of love,
Sonia Aunty

Mishki and Pushka have come to visit Earth from their home planet, Zoomba. They have never seen such an amazing place. Zoomba doesn't have trees and mountains and rivers like Earth does. But the people look exactly the same. When they come to Earth, they meet a sweet old man whom they call Daadu Dolma. Daadu Dolma shows them all the wonderful places in India and tells Mishki and Pushka all about them.

Mishki and Pushka can't believe what they see. They have seen a lot of Earth, but they have never, ever seen a place like India.

### They are off to explore India state by state :)

## Mishki

Mishki is a curious little girl. She is always asking loads of questions. On her home planet, she is always getting into trouble for poking her nose into things that are not her business.

Pushka is Mishki's brother. He loves adventure. He is always ready to try a new challenge. Whether it's climbing a mountain, or diving into a cold, cold sea, he is up for it.

## Daadu Dolma

Daadu Dolma is a wise old man who has lived on Earth longer than the mountains and seas. No one knows quite how old he is, but he certainly has been around. He knows everything about everything.

'Come on, children, get packed,' says Daadu Dolma to Mishki and Pushka.

'Why do you have such a heavy bag? Where are we going now?' asks Pushka.

'I have packed all my woollen clothes; that is why my bag is so heavy,' explains Daadu. 'You had better too. We are going to a beautiful state that can get very cold.'

Mishki jumps for joy. She loves snow. And Pushka claps his hands.

'Can we go climbing?' asks Pushka. 'Are there any mountains?'

'Oh, yes. Himachal Pradesh has the most beautiful mountains and valleys,' Daadu says. 'So get your things together quickly. It's time to go.'

Mishki and Pushka pack their bags quickly. They are

# OFF TO HIMACHAL PRADESH!!!

# Land ahoy!

That's a good observation, Mishki. But that isn't ice cream. That is snow. And those are the famous Himalayas. There are lots of hills, valleys and mountains in the beautiful state. Come, let's know more about them.

Daadu, look. Those mountains look like they are made of vanilla ice cream.

**Did you know?** The meaning of Himachal is land of snow in Sanskrit. Hima means snow and achal means land.

## BEING NEIGHBOURLY

Himachal Pradesh has a lot hilly neighbours. To its north is lovely Jammu and Kashmir, to the west is agricultural Punjab, to its east is Tibet—the roof of the world*—and to its south are Haryana and Uttarakhand. Many of these neighbours have lots of mountains and hills because they touch the Himalayas too.

To see exactly where Himachal Pradesh is on the map of India, go to http://www.mapsofindia. com/maps/india/india-political-map.htm

* Tibet is one of the highest plateaus in the world.

# HILLS AND VALLEYS

You will see lots of textures in Himachal Pradesh—lofty mountains, gentle hillsides, deep gorges that slice through them, cold lakes, terraced fields and streams and rivers with cold, clear water, rushing down mountainsides. The air is fresh and cool, and you might want to live here forever.

## AWESOME THREESOME

Himachal Pradesh has three lovely parts to it. The Shivalik range, which falls in the outer Himalayas; the central part, which has the lower or lesser Himalayas; and the northern part, which has the main or great Himalayas. This is also called the Zanskar range and has the highest mountains and the deepest valleys. Some majestic icy glaciers begin here.

# HOT AND COLD

As you climb higher, the weather gets colder. In the lower Shivalik range, summers can get pretty hot, though winters are still cold. As you go higher, the weather becomes colder and colder. By the time you reach the Greater Himalayas, it is freezing. **Brrrrrrr**! Some parts of this region have snow all year round!

Here's a house in Himachal Pradesh entirely covered in snow in February.

## ROARING RIVERS

The rivers in Himachal Pradesh hardly ever run dry. That means that they are perennial. This is because they are fed by the melting snow from the mountains. They rush down the mountains as if they are in a great hurry. The main rivers are the Sutlej, a river that is actually born in Tibet, and the Chenab (or Chandra Bhaga), which flows through the western part of the state. The other rivers that flow through this state are the Ravi, Beas, Sutlej, Yamuna and Spiti. Looks like there is no water shortage here!

Beas in Himachal

# CROP SHOP

Farming is important here and a lot of people depend on it for their livelihood. The weather is perfect for a lot of crops, like seed potatoes, mushrooms, olives, figs, ginger and other vegetables. Though this state is hilly and does not have vast plains, farmers still manage to grow some maize, rice and wheat—although not as much as in the more fertile plains.

# AN APPLE A DAY

Himachal Pradesh produces a lot of apples. Apples find the lovely climate perfect and grow nice, round and juicy. There are lots of apple orchards here and these apples find their way into homes across India.

Wow! This is so beautiful.

# FOREST FANTASY

The forests in this state are called the green pearl in the Himalayan crown. There are many types of trees in these forests. Wonderful oaks and deodars, sleek bamboos, pretty rhododendron, fir and spruce trees are just some. The government is trying to make sure that people don't cut down these forests to build homes and dams because it is important that these lovely forests be protected.

# WILD AND WONDERFUL

This state has a lot of wildlife. Some of these are rare animals on the endangered list—like the bharal (blue sheep), the Himalayan tahr and the musk deer. At higher altitudes, shepherds have claimed to have spotted the snow leopard. Other birds and animals that roam these forests are the flying squirrel, Himalayan yellow-throated marten, barking deer, rhesus macaque, Indian porcupine and many more.

# KEEPING ANIMALS SAFE

There are many sanctuaries in Himachal Pradesh, where animals can roam freely and safely, and tourists can go see them too. The Great Himalayan National Park, the Churdhar Sanctuary and the Simbalbara Sanctuary are just a few.

*Beautiful deodar forest in Manali, Himachal Pradesh*

# FUN FACTS

## State animal
Snow leopard

### State flower
Pink rhododendron

## State bird
Western tragopan

## State tree
Deodar

# WORD GRID

Eight of Himachal Pradesh's birds and animals are hiding in this grid. There are four trees too. Can you find them all? Look up to down and left to right.

| S | R | Q | W | B | A | M | B | O | O | Q | B |
|---|---|---|---|---|---|---|---|---|---|---|---|
| P | O | R | C | U | P | I | N | E | J | K | H |
| R | A | S | Q | U | I | R | R | E | L | M | A |
| U | K | W | E | D | D | F | G | H | N | M | R |
| C | F | I | R | L | E | O | P | A | R | D | A |
| E | Z | X | C | V | E | B | N | M | K | L | L |
| W | T | T | H | A | R | D | D | E | E | R | J |
| Q | A | S | M | A | C | A | Q | U | E | E | R |

# CHARMING CITIES

The cities of Himachal Pradesh are different from most other cities in India. Because the climate is mostly cold and because many of these cities are high up in the mountains, they look different from cities on the plains. Let's visit some of them.

## SHIMLA

This lovely city is the state capital. It was also the summer capital of the British, when they ruled India. They built many of the homes and buildings that make Shimla so lovely.

## DHARAMSHALA

Dharamshala (or Dharamsala) is the second capital of Himachal Pradesh. Its original name was Bhagsu. It is a beautiful city and super important because the great Tibetan spiritual leader Dalai Lama's home is here.

## KULLU

This is a lovely little valley town that sits right on the edge of the Beas. The town of Manali smiles down at it.

## MANALI

This is a beautiful little town that tourists love. It sits on the edge of the Beas valley. There are lots of adventure sports you can try here—paragliding, mountaineering, hiking and river rafting.

# DALHOUSIE

This hill station was built by the British for their troops to live in during summer. It was named after Lord Dalhousie. It is full of colonial bungalows and churches that the British built.

## KASAULI

Here's another charming British-built town. It is also called a cantonment town, which means it has a large army base, where many army officers live with their families.

# HIDDEN WORDS

Look at the name of this lovely city. How many smaller words can you make from it? Mishki has made five. Can you make more than she has?

## DALHOUSIE

HOUSE _____    _____    _____

_____    _____    _____

_____    _____    _____

# Long, long ago

Daadu, they say mountains are really old—older than mankind. So, Himachal Pradesh must have a long history too!

Yes, you are right. It does. This state's history can be traced back to millions of years.

The Vedas were written in Sanskrit.

The Vedas are old, old writings that tell us about how life was thousands of years ago.

## MILLIONS OF YEARS AGO

Around 5000 years ago, at the foothills of the Himalayas, lived the people belonging to the Indus Valley Civilization. The Vedas call these people the Daasas, or Daasyus. Still other texts call them Kols and Mundas. These people lived peacefully in this lush land for many centuries.

# A NEW WAVE OF MIGRANTS

From Central Asia, a group of people made their way to the foothills of the Himalayas and pushed aside the people already living here. These invaders had Mongoloid features. They were called the Bhotas and Kiratas.

Migrants coming to India

# THE ARYANS ARRIVE

The Daasas were pushed aside by the Aryans, who also came into India through the passes in the mountains. The Aryans were strong and spread themselves over a large part of India. In fact, they formed the base of a lot of India's recorded history.

## RHYME AWAY

Pushka wants to write a poem about the strong Aryans. Help him find rhyming words for

# STRONG

_____ _____

_____ _____

_____ _____

## TRIBAL TRACTS

The region that is now Himachal Pradesh was, in those days, made of many small units, each of which was like a mini kingdom. These were called *Janpadas*. They had their own leaders and their own culture. And naturally, they had their own names too, like Trigarta, Kuluta, Audumbras and Kulindas. They happily coexisted till Chandragupta arrived.

*Chandragupta Maurya invaded Himachal.*

# THE MAURYA EMPIRE

Chandragupta Maurya conquered a lot of India. He overcame Himachal's peace-loving communities too. His grandson Emperor Ashoka took over conquering land after land. This went on until he saw so much bloodshed that he decided to give up war and become a Buddhist.

*King Ashoka built a stupa in Kullu valley.*

# CHIEFTAINS' RULE

*Harshavardhana was a strong ruler.*

Emperor Ashoka began to lose interest in his kingdom and soon it collapsed. The part that is Himachal was taken over by small chieftains called the Thakurs and the Ranas. When the strong King Harshavardhana rose to power, these rulers submitted to his supremacy.

# RISE OF THE RAJPUTS

By the time Harshavardhana died, the Rajput clans started expanding their kingdoms. They found this magical land and spread their control here too! They broke this region up into tiny states with names like Bilaspur, Kangra, Mandi and Suket.

Rajputs made their home in Himachal.

# MIXED-UP WORDS

Pushka is trying to remember what he's learnt. But he has mixed up the words. Help him un-jumble them.

The **TRAJUPS** _____ ruled after King Harshavardhana.

**KAAOSH** _____ was a great king who became a Buddhist.

The **NAVARS** _____ pushed aside the Mongols.

The **AYRUAM** _____ Empire spread to a large part of India.

# STRONG DYNASTIES

Many conquerors had their eye on this lovely land. A man called Mahmud Ghazni conquered Kangra. Other Muslim rulers, like Timur and Sikander Lodi, captured the forts the Rajputs and other clans had built. In the meantime, the Mughals had taken control over a large part of India. They made their presence felt here too!

Timur was a strong and ruthless king.

## BACK TO LOCAL RULE

Soon, the Mughal dynasty became weak, as the kings began to pay less attention to this far-flung place. The local leaders found the perfect opportunity to break free. A local king, Maharaja Sansar Chand, took over. He ruled for nearly half a century and under his rule the region prospered.

A Gorkha king

Even today, the Gorkhas are an army regiment in the Indian army.

## A STRONG TRIBE!

The Gorkhas were a strong tribe who were particularly good at warfare. They had come to power in neighbouring Nepal. They defeated Maharaja Sansar Chand and began to rule over this part of Himachal Pradesh. But they were not too successful in either retaining or expanding their rule. They had a huge battle with the British, who were slowly taking over India.

# BRITISH TAKE OVER

The British had, by this time, begun to rule over the whole of India. The simple peace-loving mountain folk of this region stayed under British rule. During this time, there were many smaller hilly kingdoms. All of them were loyal to the British crown. Much of this area developed because the British loved the climate here. But slowly, the entire country of India started struggling to get the British to leave them alone. And so, after much struggle, in 1947 India became independent.

The British took over Himachal.

# HIMACHAL PRADESH, AT LAST!

In the beginning, immediately after Independence, this state was called the Himachal Pradesh Province. It had many smaller kings. It was only in 1970, after a lot of changes, that the state became Himachal Pradesh, as we know it today.

Did you know?
Himachal Pradesh was a Union Territory from after Independence till it was declared a state in 1970.

Whew! Such a long history for such a small state!

Talk time

Daadu, can we go and talk to the people of this state? They sound really interesting.

Yes, of course. But first, do you want to know a little bit about the language they speak? You will find it easier to talk to them.

Let's see some words in Chambali (you will find it is rather close to Hindi).

- Hello = Namaste
- Goodbye = Asi chale
- Thank you = Dhanyavad
- What is your name? = Tumhara na kya hai?
- My name is Pushka. = Mere na hai Pushka.
- How much does this cost? = Iseri kya kimat hai?
- Where are you going? = Tussi kute hin chale re?
- Happy birthday = Janam din di shubh kaamna
- Small = Nikka
- Big = Badda
- I need help = Tussi meri madad karo

The main language people speak here is Hindi. But there are many dialects that have come down through the years. Some of these are Pahari, Dogri, Kangri, Kinnauri and Chambali. Some people speak Punjabi and many words are common too!

LINGO
SHINGO

Pushka wants to practise the new language. Can you help him match the English words to the Chambali words?

| Goodbye | How much does this cost? | Small | Big | Where are you going? |

| Badda | Nikka | Asi chale | Tusi kute hin chale re? | Iseri kya kimat hai? |

# A peep into their life

Daadu! Many of the people here have unusual features. Why is that?

You see, Tibetans, Mongols and others married local people. Their children developed mixed features. That's why their features are slightly different.

## A LOVELY MIX

The people who live in Himachal Pradesh are a mixed bunch. That's because, for over thousands of years, different kinds of people have all left a little bit of their lifestyles and habits behind. The local people have community names like Gujari, Pangwali, Kinnauri or Lahuli. Many people from Punjab have settled here in this lovely state. Though most people here are Hindu, there are a lot of Buddhists here as well! And like the rest of India, there are Muslims, Christians and Sikhs who call this state home.

# CHREWAL

This is a month-long festival that is also called Prithvi Pooja (praying to earth). It is celebrated during August. Through this month, farmers do not work their oxen. Girls put together lovely dances and there are flowers everywhere.

# HARYALI

This festival is celebrated on 16 July, with the first rains. Pests like bugs and fleas that destroy crops are destroyed ceremoniously, in cow-dung balls. Then people gather in a village square, garland the gods with wildflowers, thank the gods for all that they have and pray for a good harvest. Farmers give their oxen a good rest on this day. Women get together and sing and dance for Haryali Teej.

Swinging gaily during Teej is great fun!

# KULLU DUSSEHRA

When India finishes celebrating the festival of Dussehra, the grand Dussehra festival in Kullu begins. For seven days, the people in the valley get together to pray, celebrate, sing, dance and eat amazing food. There are food stalls and shops on the roads, and there is a grand procession during which the idols of Raghunathji (the local god) and Hidimba (the local goddess) are carried through the streets with much song and dance.

# PHULECH

This is a flower festival that is celebrated just before the rainy months. People from every family go off to the hills to collect lots of wild flowers. They make lovely garlands with these, which are placed on the village deity. The head priest then makes a prediction about the rains and the kind of crops that the land will be blessed with.

# LOSAR

This is a fun fifteen-day festival that is held in either January or February—not just in this state but across many Himalayan regions. It is basically the Tibetan new year, which all the Buddhists here celebrate with much gusto. They do a fun mask dance and eat yummy soup with dumplings in it, with noodles called *guthuk*. People wear traditional costumes and light firecrackers too!

Looks like fun!

# SHIVRATRI

People in this state are big worshippers of Shiva. During this festival, people fast and sing songs in praise of Shiva and his wife Parvati. Thousands of people collect in temples to sing, pray and dance. Mandi is the place where the grandest of Shivratri celebrations is held.

Shivratri is a big celebration here.

Pushka loves festivals. He also loves puzzles. Help him crack these clues about the festivals in Himachal Pradesh.

## ACROSS

1. In the Phulech festival, the priest foretells the kind of _____ the land will be blessed with.

5. The festival which is the grandest in Mandi.

7. The wife of Lord Shiva.

8. During the Tibetan new year, people do this fun dance.

9. The name of the festival that celebrates the Tibetan new year.

## DOWN

2. Something cold and wet that helps water the crops.

3. The month-long festival during which the oxen get their rest.

4. The festival that celebrates the first rains.

6. The god to whom people pray, along with his wife.

# CHANCE TO DANCE

There are many enjoyable and unusual dance styles in Himachal Pradesh. People are fun-loving and love to dance. Let's see some really good ones.

## KULLU NATI

This lovely dance is performed in the Kullu Valley—especially during the Dussehra festival. People wear traditional costumes and dance till they are exhausted. They dance to musical instruments like the *narsingha*, *shehnai*, dhol and nagara.

## CHHANAK CHHAM

This charming dance is performed as a tribute to Buddha. The dancers wear headgear called *chhanak*. They move in a slow circle while musicians play long pipes called *tangchim* and drums called *ghhan*.

## THODA DANCE

This is a war dance that people once performed as a ritual before troops went into battle. The dancers wave bows and arrows or swords and dance in dramatic movements. Must be exciting to do, but be careful with the weapons!

I'm going to learn these dances!

## LOSAR SHONA CHUKSAM

This dance is performed in the Kinnaur region during the Losar festival. The musical instruments used during this dance are the dhol, *bugjal* (bronze cymbals), *karnal* (a long windpipe) and *ransingha* (a curved trumpet).

# FUN AT THE FAIR

Himachal Pradesh has lots of fairs too that are a lot of fun! People dress up, collect in large numbers and have a blast together. They buy and sell things and, for a while, forget all their worries.

## THE LAVI FAIR

In the olden days, people in Tibet and Kinnaur traded many things. They would get together on a certain day and do all their business. That tradition remains, and for three days during October or November, people from all over the state collect in a place called Rampur Bushahr. They bring with them their mules, horses, yaks, woollen clothes, dry fruit and other goods to buy and sell. All through the day, people trade goods. At night, they sing and dance around bonfires and eat yummy food.

*Wild flowers in Rohtang Pass*

## THE PHUL YATRA FAIR

When winter comes to the mountains, everything is covered in snow and people have to stay indoors. They pray to a local goddess and have a good time before the snow brings everything to a halt. They sing joyfully and do the mask and lion dance that is so famous in this area.

# THE CHINTPURNI FAIR

The local people call this fair Mata-da-mela (Mother Goddess' fair). The story goes that a goddess appeared before a woman and asked her to perform a puja (prayer) to bring prosperity to her home for all generations to come. From that day on, this became an annual affair. People pray to the Mother Goddess for eight days. On the eighth day, they make a delicious dish called *karahi* and offer it to the goddess before eating some themselves.

Chintpurni Devi's Durbar in Himachal

## YAKKETY YAK!

Pushka wants to see a yak at the Lavi fair. Can you help him spot the shadow of this yak?

# Bricks and stones

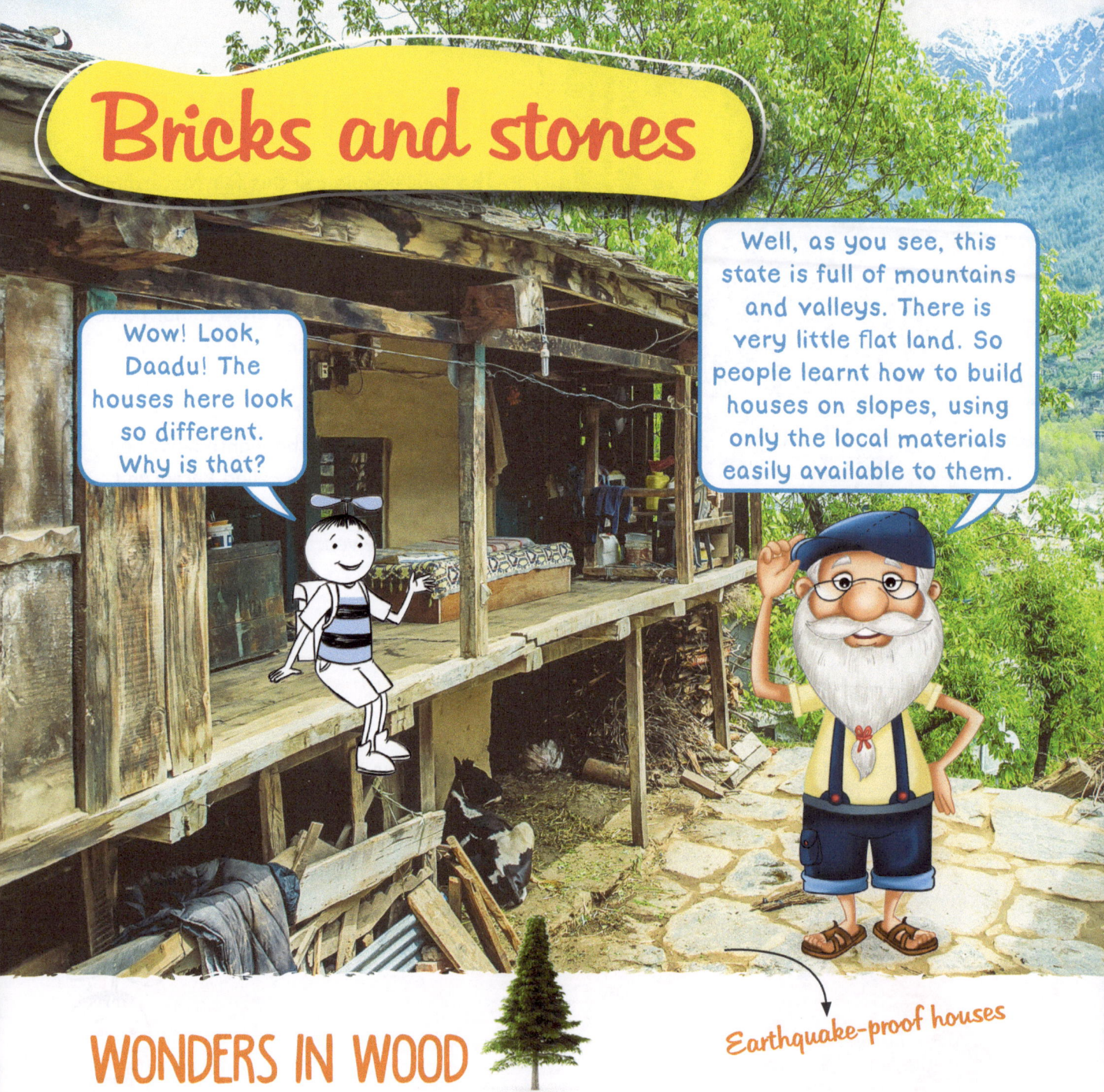

Wow! Look, Daadu! The houses here look so different. Why is that?

Well, as you see, this state is full of mountains and valleys. There is very little flat land. So people learnt how to build houses on slopes, using only the local materials easily available to them.

Earthquake-proof houses

## WONDERS IN WOOD

Since a lot of this state is covered with forests, wood has always been the main material for building houses. Not just that! This region is also very prone to earthquakes. That is why people make sure houses are light, so even if they come crashing down in an earthquake, no one gets hurt. The wood from deodar and kail trees were the best for construction. People also used stone wherever they needed a material that would last in rain and snow.

## LIVING IN CLUSTERS

Here's something you will see in the villages of Himachal Pradesh. The houses are built in tight clusters, around a tiny village square. The temple is always at the centre of all action and is at the highest point of the village.

Houses built in tight clusters

This is so amazing!

The roof is always sloping to help the snow slide off. Isn't that clever?

A rural house

## KATHKUNI HOUSES

The people here are clever. They have developed a type of house that is perfect for their lifestyle. It is called *kathkuni*. It is made of wood, stone and mud. Usually, they have two or three floors. The lowest floor is used to house sheep and cattle. The kitchen, bedrooms and other living spaces are on the first and second floors. Many of these houses also have balconies, where the family sits and enjoys the fabulous view.

# INSIDE A KATHKUNI HOUSE

The people here don't bother too much with heavy furniture. They simply make storage within the walls itself. Instead of heavy beds, they use mats made of goat hair called *kahayrcha*. And they store all the other household stuff in simple chests or trunks. Many houses have a hearth in the middle of the room. They light a cosy fire and sit around it to stay warm through the cold winter evenings.

*What a clever way to store things!*

*There's no need for complicated furniture.*

# COLONIAL SPLENDOUR

The British loved the climate in Himachal Pradesh. They developed many villages into large towns. They built the typical British houses that are in a colonial style—that is, much like the houses they had back home in England. But even they used as much local material as possible. Many of these houses or bungalows look like chalets and homes in other mountain countries, like Switzerland. **How cool!**

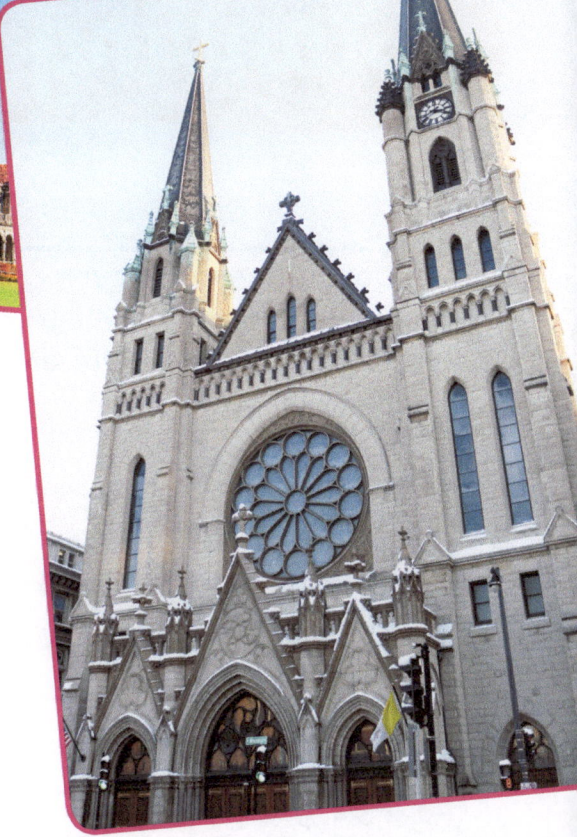

# GRAND BUILDINGS

Shimla, the capital of Himachal Pradesh, was the summer capital for the British, who ruled India for so many years. When the rest of India was too hot for them, they retreated to Shimla with their families. They built not just homes but offices too. Many of these are now used to house government offices. They also built lots of churches that are exactly like the ones they left behind in England.

## RHYME TIME

It is so much fun to rhyme!

Pushka is so inspired by the houses here that he has made a poem. Can you help him complete the rhyme?

People here are so smart,

The houses they build are a work of _____

They're built of bamboo and of wood

They are strong and they look so _____

The people stay fine if the houses shake

They're built to stay safe in an earth _____

33

# Standing strong

Daadu, there are such unusual-looking buildings here. And so many different types too! What are they?

Well, Himachal Pradesh is very different from other Indian states. Different kinds of people lived here and they built monuments. Come, let's see some of these wonderful monuments.

## THE MAGNIFICENT KANGRA FORT

This amazing fort is one of the oldest and largest in the Himalayan region. It was built by the Rajput kings. It was captured at different times by different kings—first by the ruthless Mahmud Ghazni, then Muhammed bin Tughlaq (of the Delhi Sultanate) and then the Mughals. It passed on from ruler to ruler, till the British finally arrived. It has awesome entry gates, many temples and one of India's most beautiful palaces inside.

# THE GENTLE KAMRU FORT

The Kamru Fort was built by a local king called Dev Puran. It's high on a mountain top. It is full of beautiful wooden carvings. This doesn't at all look like the fearsome forts that Mughals built, but is a gentler collection of houses, surrounded by orchards. There is a temple to Kamakhya Devi, the goddess after whom the temple is named. You sure can't imagine fierce battles being fought at this fort.

# THE FORT OF PAINTINGS— THE SUJANPUR FORT

Aha! This one looks a little more like the forts we imagine. It was built by a king called Raja Abhaya Chand of Kangra. Later, Raja Sansar Chand, who loved miniature paintings, lived here. He filled the palace fort with lovely paintings and spent a lot of time here. There are Shiva temples inside the fort. You can still imagine how the raja lived in those faraway days.

**Did you know?**
This lovely fort was destroyed by a fire and then an earthquake—so a lot of it is in ruins.

# MAHARAJA'S PALACE IN CHAIL

This lovely palace has a story behind it. A king named Maharaja Bhupinder Singh had a spat with a British official. He was expelled from Shimla, where he had a palace. He was so angry that he decided to build an even better palace. He built a palace in Chail, in which he lived royally. Many, many years later, when his descendants found it difficult to maintain, it was turned into a hotel. It looks more like a grand old mansion, but a palace it certainly is!

# RANG MAHAL

This gorgeous palace was built by a king called Raja Umed Singh. It is called the 'Painted Palace' because it is full of lovely paintings of Lord Krishna and his life. It is a mix of different types of architecture—colonial and Indian. Now, it is a hotel, so you can actually go live there and pretend that you are a raja!

This is so beautiful

# CHRIST CHURCH

Right at the heart of Shimla is the mall (an open marketplace). It's where everyone collects and where all the action is. Christ Church is a pale-yellow church, situated in the mall, and is believed to be one of the oldest churches in North India. They say it took more than ten years to build. Over the years, different people added to its beauty. Everyone who visits Shimla is bound to see this lovely old church standing in the middle of the city.

# THE VICEREGAL LODGE

This lovely house used to be where the viceroy lived. It is full of beautiful galleries, halls, fireplaces, ballrooms, terraces and verandas. It even has an indoor tennis court! Imagine that! It was the first building in Himachal Pradesh to get electricity. When the British were there, there would be glittering parties where Indian maharajas would rub shoulders with British aristocracy. It was very politically important too. This was where the British and Indian leaders met for an important meeting called the Simla Conference (Shimla used to be called Simla at that time).

This is where it was decided that India would be divided into India and Pakistan.

## SPOT THE DIFFERENCE

Mishki has drawn a church. And so has Pushka. But there are ten differences between the two pictures.

Can you spot them all?

# HIDIMBA TEMPLE

This is one of the oldest temples in the area. It is the temple of Hidimba, who was the wife of Bhim (the second Pandava brother). She was believed to be a gentle giantess, who prayed to goddess Durga to forgive her for her sins. Durga was so pleased that she made her into a goddess too! There is a huge footprint, which people believe is Hidimba's footprint.

# ROCK-CUT TEMPLES

This is a group of fifteen temples cut out of rock with lots of detailed carvings on them. You can just imagine how hard it was to carve on stone in the olden days, when people had no high-tech tools. Standing for years and years near the region called Kangra, these temples have carvings of Lord Rama, his wife Sita and Lord Shiva too.

# KI GOMPA MONASTERY

This is the name of a famous Buddhist monastery in the Spiti valley that is more than a thousand years old. It was founded by a monk named Dromton and lamas came there to study Buddhist teachings and meditate. There are many murals and paintings of Gautam Buddha. The monastery was destroyed by invaders several times, but every time, Buddhist believers stubbornly rebuilt it.

The entire region of Spiti is called Little Tibet because its culture is very similar to Tibet's.

# TABO MONASTERY

It feels so calm here.

There was once a Buddhist king called Yeshe O'd, who lived thousands of years ago. He, his sons and nephews built this lovely monastery near the region of Spiti. The monastery was a great centre of learning where Buddhist monks and philosophers met, discussed religion and spread Buddhism. There are many paintings and carvings throughout the monastery that give us a peep into the life of the monks and into Buddhist beliefs. It sure is a calm place where you feel very good!

## TWIN MONKS

Mishki and Pushka met many monks during their visit to the Tabo monastery. Two of the monks were twins. Can you figure out which two are exactly alike?

A    B    C    D    E

# Working hard

I would LOVE to live in this lovely state. It must be so relaxing—spending all day just looking at the lovely views of valleys and mountains.

Well, Mishki! Of course the mountains are beautiful, but people have to work very hard to earn a living. It's not easy living up in the mountains. Come, let me tell you what people in these hills do for a living.

## FARMER, FARMER WHAT DO YOU GROW?

The farmers in this state are very busy people. They grow lots of things. Not just regular crops like maize and rice, which are not plentiful. They also grow lots of apples and work hard in apple orchards. They work in the fields to grow seed potatoes, mushrooms, figs, olives, ginger and all kinds of vegetables.

## MINDING SHEEP AND COWS

Breeding sheep and cows for different products, like milk and wool, is also important. There are lots of people who work in this business that is called animal husbandry.

## RHYME TIME

Mishki loves the figs that grow in Himachal Pradesh. She is trying to make a poem but needs five more words that rhyme with fig. Can you help her out?

# FIG

_____   _____

_____   _____

_____   _____

## POWER FROM WATER

We all know that we need a lot of electricity to run our lives. Did you know that a lot of India's hydro-electricity (that is electricity got from the force of water) comes from Himachal Pradesh? Thanks to the gushing force of rivers coming tumbling down mountainsides, there are many hydro-electric plants where many people work hard at providing electricity.

# HANDY HANDICRAFTS

The people of Himachal Pradesh seem to be truly talented. For generations, they have been creating the most intricate and colourful objects in wood, leather, metal and stone. Let's see some of what these amazing craftsmen do.

# WEAVING MAGIC

The carpets, rugs and blankets from the mountains of Himachal Pradesh are famous everywhere. These weavers create wonderful designs with dragons, swastikas and trees in blossom. Many of these are made from the wool of a special breed of mountain sheep called Giangi sheep.

The blankets that the weavers here make are called *gudma*.

# TOURISTY TRENDS

With so much to see and do, tourists from all over the world flock to this state. There are many, many hotels, lots of shops and markets, and hundreds of big and small restaurants in which people work. In fact, people from other states come and work here as well, so that they can enjoy the lovely state while they work.

Wouldn't it be fun to drink hot tea on a cold day here?

# NATTY NEEDLEWORK

The women here love their embroidery and are very skilled at it too! They embroider beautiful scarves, caps, clothes, gloves and a whole lot of other things. The tradition of embroidering handkerchiefs (called rumals) must be over a thousand years old. All these lovely pieces are sold in local markets and exported all over the world too!

# A SPECIAL KIND OF JEWELLERY

When the Rajputs ruled this region, they favoured a special kind of jewellery for which the people of Kullu, Manali and Chamba were famous. Even now, these craftsmen make the most wondrous silver, metal and enamel jewellery that tourists are crazy about.

Silver jewellery of Himachal

# WHAT'S ODD?

In each row below, there's one word that's odd. Pushka can't seem to figure it out. Can you circle them?

| KULLU | MANALI | BANGALORE | CHAMBA |

| SILVER | METAL | LEATHER | ENAMEL |

| CARPET | RUG | BLANKET | BOTTLE |

# Yum yum yum

I'm tired, Daadu. I feel like I have climbed mountains. Now I'm terribly hungry. What do I get to eat here?

You've only read about the mountains. What will you do when you actually climb them? Well, anyway, I can definitely tell you what kind of amazing food you will get to eat here. So get ready for a treat.

## THREE MEALS MAKE A DAY

In Himachal Pradesh, there are many hill tribes who cook food in their own special way. Some eat more rice, while others choose rotis. The three main traditional meals are breakfast (*nuhari*), lunch (*dhupahari*) and an evening meal (*sanhiyalu*). Rotis are made of corn and barley. And, of course, come festivals, the state turns into a food heaven. The most unique thing about Himachali food is that it changes from region to region within the state. **So much variety!**

Gulgule are sweet fritters made during celebrations. Polu pakodu are more savoury snacks made during times of fasting.

# SIDU

This is a yummy bread that is first baked and then steamed. That's not all. A dollop of butter or ghee on it and you can have it along with a mutton curry or even a dal.

*Dham being prepared*

# DHAM

*Dham* is a traditional Himachali festival meal. A typical dham includes rice, moong dal and a dish of rajma or chana (cooked with curd), followed by mash dal, khatta (a sweet and sour sauce) and ends with mitha bhaat or sweet rice. Traditionally, dham is cooked by *botis* (Himachali Brahmins).

## Crack the code

Mishki is telling Daadu something in a code language. Can you crack the code and see what she is trying to say?

| U = 1 | D = 2 | I = 3 | S = 4 | A = 5 | E = 6 |
|-------|-------|-------|-------|-------|-------|
| T = 7 | O = 8 | N = 9 | W = 0 | | |

3 0 5 9 7    7 8    7 5 4 7 6    5    4 3 2 1

__ __ __ __ __   __ __   __ __ __ __ __   __   __ __ __ __

# BHEY

Guess what this unusual dish is made from? Yes! The stem of the lotus flower. These stems are thick and when they are cut and fried with amazing masalas, they taste heavenly.

# BABRU

This is the Himalayan cousin of the popular kachori of Uttar Pradesh. It is a fried dumpling stuffed to bursting with black gram paste. Have it with the lip-smacking tamarind chutney. **Yummmmm!**

Lotus stems are eaten with relish in some other states too. Of course, the way they are cooked is quite different.

# CHHA GOSHT

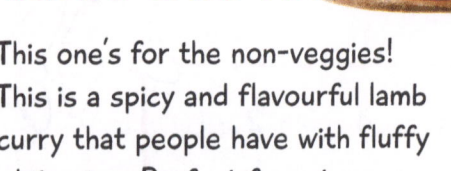

This one's for the non-veggies! This is a spicy and flavourful lamb curry that people have with fluffy white rice. Perfect for a tummy that's hungry.

# AKOTRI

Time for something sweet! Akotri is a delicious cake that is healthy too! It is made during festivals and celebrations, and you certainly can eat a lot of it.

That's how yummy it is.

# PATANDE

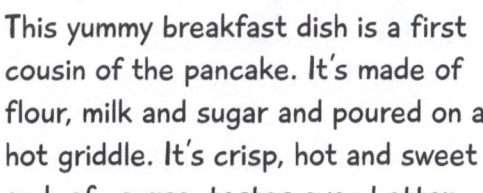

This yummy breakfast dish is a first cousin of the pancake. It's made of flour, milk and sugar and poured on a hot griddle. It's crisp, hot and sweet and, of course, tastes even better with a dollop of ghee.

# FOODIE GRID

Pushka is very hungry. All the yummy food of Himachal Pradesh is hidden in this grid. Help him find it all. There are eight dishes hidden here.

| U | P | A | T | A | N | D | E | B | A |
|---|---|---|---|---|---|---|---|---|---|
| B | H | E | Y | Y | T | R | E | W | Q |
| I | O | O | A | K | O | T | R | I | Q |
| B | A | B | R | U | Y | T | R | E | W |
| Q | A | S | D | F | G | S | I | D | U |
| W | D | H | A | M | Y | U | I | O | P |
| E | R | T | G | U | G | U | L | E | L |
| C | H | H | A | G | O | S | H | T | G |

# What to wear?

Wow! Look, Daadu! Are those women dressed for a party? Their long dresses are so lovely!

No, Mishki. That is what women wear here. The traditional clothes in the hills of Himachal Pradesh are different from what people wear in much of India. Let me tell you why!

## DRESSED FOR THE COLD

The weather in this lovely state can be freezing at times. This is why people have developed a style of clothing that helps them stay warm. Also, there are so many types of tribes and regions which have their own style of dressing.

## PRETTY IN A PATTU

To stay warm in the cold, cold weather, women (and sometimes men too) wear a thick, colourful shawl called a *pattu*. It is draped around the body and fastened with a pin or a brooch. It sure keeps you warm.

# LOVELY IN LAHAUL

The men of a region called Lahaul choose to wear long woollen gowns over trousers. Their boots are made of grass or leather and are designed to keep the snow out. They also wear caps and the style of their cap tells people exactly where they are from.

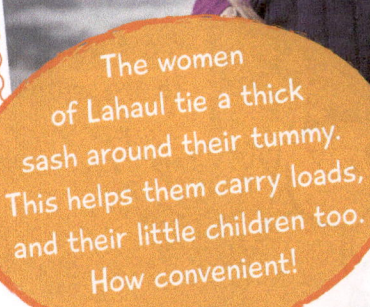

The women of Lahaul tie a thick sash around their tummy. This helps them carry loads, and their little children too. How convenient!

# DIFFERENT STROKES

The Brahmins, on the other hand, wore a completely different style of clothes. A dhoti with a kurta and a waistcoat was their traditional outfit. The Rajputs wore tight pants called churidar and a long coat. A starched turban completed the grand outfit.

# GADDI STYLE

The women of a tribe called Gaddi wear a lot of jewellery. They wear silver, beads, corals and many rows of semi-precious stones. They even wear peacock feathers as ornaments.

The men wear an unusual cap with a peak. People say the peak of the cap is supposed to be a symbol of the Mount Kailash peak in the Himalayas. The cap has flaps that cover their ears when it's freezing.

# Autograph, please?

Daadu, this is quite a tiny state. Are there many famous people here?

Oh, Mishki! The size of a place has nothing to do with how great its people can be. Himachal Pradesh has produced some very famous people. Some of them were born here and some chose to make this state their home. Come, let's meet some of them.

## DALAI LAMA

This great man doesn't belong to Himachal Pradesh but to the whole world. Though he was born in Tibet, because he had to go into political exile, he made his home in Dharamshala, Himachal Pradesh. He is a great Buddhist leader who spreads the message of the Buddha across the world.

# CAPTAIN VIKRAM BATRA

He was a brave war hero who gave his life for India during the terrible Kargil war. He was awarded India's highest honour, the Param Vir Chakra.

# CHARANJIT SINGH

He was India's hockey captain who led the Indian hockey team to win the silver and gold medals in the Olympics in two different years.

# KINKRI DEVI

You would never recognize her if you saw her, but this simple mountain woman is known all over the world for the way she fought to preserve the environment against mining and other activities that destroy the mountains of Himachal Pradesh.

# DALIP  SINGH RANA

He is better known as the Great Khali, the wrestler who has become popular all over the world for his strength and skills in the WWE shows.

# NIRMAL VERMA

Nirmal Verma was a famous Hindi writer and novelist. He is considered to be one of the pioneers of the 'Nayi Kahaani' movement in Hindi literature. He has been awarded the Sahitya Akademi Award and the Padma Bhushan.

# PREITY ZINTA

This charming actor has appeared in lots of very popular Hindi movies.

# VIJAY KUMAR

This army man has won a silver medal in shooting in the Olympics. He has served his country in sport and in defence too! That makes him super special.

## Olympic Challenge

Pushka wants to become famous too, by taking part in the Olympics. He is practising shooting but has lost the target. Can you help him reach the centre of the target?

# Once upon a time . . .

Daadu, these mountains must have many stories hidden in them. Can you tell us one?

A GRAIN OF SEED

Yes, certainly. There are many folk stories that the mountain people tell their children on cold winter nights. Come, I will tell you one.

There was once a man who lived high up on a mountainside in Chamba. He lived with his three sons, Batu, Satu and Natu. He had lost his wife years ago. He was a simple shepherd and made his living caring for his sheep and goats. He taught his sons the art of shepherding. The small family lived off the wool they sold. It was a hard life.

One day, the father was very ill. He was very old and knew his end was near. He called his three sons to him and said, 'Sons, I will not be with you for much longer. But before I go, I am giving you a small treasure.' Batu's and Satu's eyes lit up. They were lazy, greedy, good-for-nothing boys. But Natu loved his father. His eyes filled with tears.

'Oh, Baba, don't speak like that,' he said tearfully. The old man smiled and held out his hand. There were three seeds in it.

'Is that the treasure?' Batu exclaimed. He took his seed and threw it in the drain, where it got washed away.

'Oh, is that all?' said Satu scornfully. He grabbed the seed and put it on a shelf, and there it lay forgotten.

But Natu, the youngest son, took the seed gratefully. He planted it in the backyard. Soon their father passed away.

A few weeks later, Batu and Satu came to speak to Natu.

'Natu, we have decided to give up shepherding. We don't like it. We will go to Shimla and work in the city. We will get jobs and earn lots of money,' they told him. 'You can stay behind and look after sheep and goats. We will be rich.'

'But Baba wanted all of us to stay in our home,' protested Natu, but to no avail. His brothers' minds were made up. They left Natu all alone in the mountain village with his sheep and goats.

Seasons passed. Soon winter came and the snows swirled down the slopes. Natu had gone down to the warmth of the valley, with the other villagers. He had almost nothing left. He could not manage to look after the sheep and goats without his brothers and had sold them. But he was determined not to leave his father's home.

When winter changed to summer and flowers began to peep out in the grass, it was time to go back up. Natu trudged up the mountainside to the little house he had lived in all his life. When he reached there, he stared in horror. The snow and rats had completely destroyed the house. There was nothing left.

Natu sat down with head in his hands. What was he going to do? He had no sheep, no goats and now he had no home either.

Just then, from the corner of his eye, he saw a brave green plant that seemed to be calling out to him.

*I wonder what that is*, he thought. He went to take a closer look. It was the seed his father had given him. It had turned into a plant.

Natu smiled. Here, at least, was a memory of his father. He watered it and saw it grow. The plant grew into a strong vine. It began to spread out with wide green leaves and bright yellow flowers. Just looking at it cheered Natu up. After some time, the flowers turned into fruit. Big, heavy, orange fruit.

Natu cut the large fruit and cooked it with wheat and sattu. It was delicious.

Soon, Natu had hundreds of these magical fruit all around him. He began to sell the fruit. He made more money than he ever had before.

He thought back to what his father had said—there truly was a treasure hidden in the seed. The treasure was a pumpkin.

This is the story of how pumpkins found their way to Himachal Pradesh. People say that as long as there are pumpkins, the people of Himachal will never go hungry.

# TRAVEL DIARY

Have you enjoyed this trip to Himachal Pradesh with your friends Mishki and Pushka—and, of course, with Daadu Dolma?

Now you can make your own Himachal Pradesh diary. And if you ever visit Himachal Pradesh, make sure you take pictures and put them in the photo box.

The first place I would visit in Himachal Pradesh:

_____

If I were in Himachal Pradesh, I would be a part of this festival:

_____

The one dish I am definitely going to eat:

_____

The monument I think is the most interesting:

_____

The one famous person from Himachal Pradesh I would love to meet:

_____

If I were from Himachal Pradesh, I would do this dance:

_____

The festival from Himachal Pradesh that I think is the most fun:

_____

The five words that I think describe Himachal Pradesh the best are:

_____

_____

_____

_____

_____

My Himachal Pradesh memories:

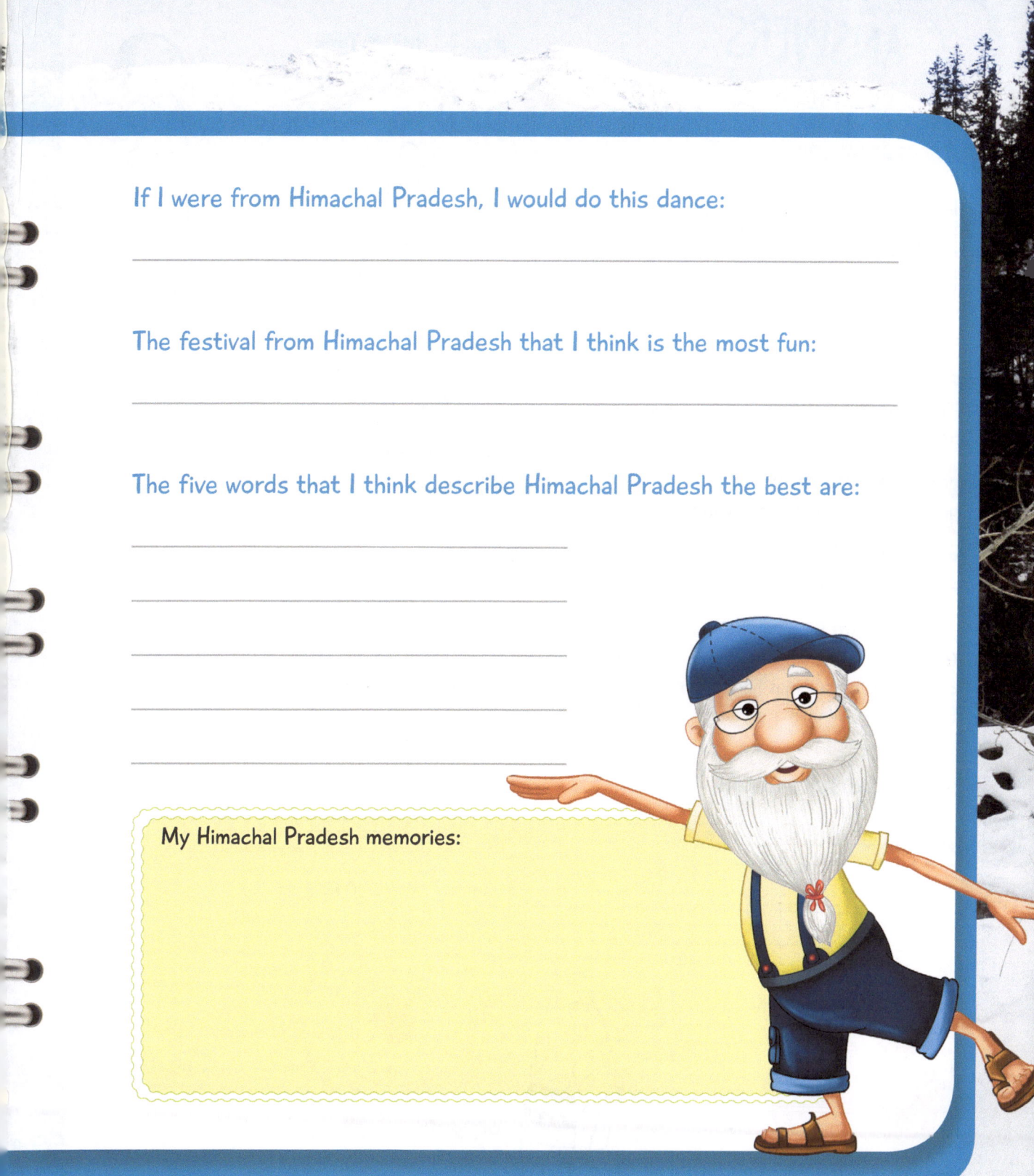

# ANSWERS

## page 11 WORD GRID

| S | R | Q | W | B | A | M | B | O | O | Q | B |
| P | O | R | C | U | P | I | N | E | J | K | H |
| R | A | S | Q | U | I | R | R | E | L | M | A |
| U | K | W | E | D | D | F | G | H | N | M | R |
| C | F | I | R | L | E | O | P | A | R | D | A |
| E | Z | X | C | V | E | B | N | M | K | L | L |
| W | T | T | H | A | R | D | D | E | E | R | J |
| Q | A | S | M | A | C | A | Q | U | E | E | R |

## page 13 HIDDEN WORDS

Here are some of the words you can form:
house, do, ale, louse, sad, had, lad, side

## page 15 RHYME AWAY

gong, long, song, prong, wrong

## page 17 MIXED-UP WORDS

RAJPUTS, ASHOKA, ARYANS, MAURYA

## page 21 LINGO SHINGO

Goodbye—Asi chale; How much does this cost?—Iseri kya kimat hai?; Small—Nikka; Big—Badda; Where are you going?—Tusi kute hin chale re?

## page 25 CROSSWORD TIME

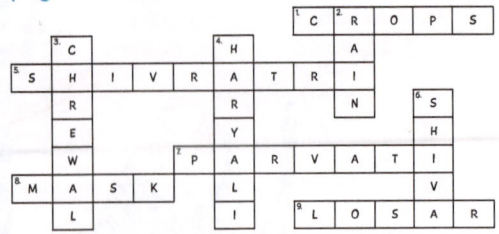

## page 29 YAKKETY YAK!

## page 33 RHYME TIME

Art, good, quake

## page 37 SPOT THE DIFFERENCE

## page 39 TWIN MONKS

A and B are twins.

## page 41 RHYME TIME

big, dig, gig, jig, pig, rig, sprig, swig, wig, zig

## page 43 WHAT'S ODD?

BANGALORE, LEATHER, BOTTLE

## page 45 CRACK THE CODE

I WANT TO TASTE A SIDU

## page 47 FOODIE GRID

| U | P | A | T | A | N | D | E | B | A |
| B | H | E | Y | Y | T | R | E | W | Q |
| I | O | O | A | K | O | T | R | I | Q |
| B | A | B | R | U | Y | Y | T | R | E | W |
| Q | A | S | D | F | G | S | I | D | U |
| W | D | H | A | M | Y | U | I | O | P |
| E | R | T | G | U | G | U | L | E | L |
| C | H | H | A | G | O | S | H | T | G |

## page 53 OLYMPIC CHALLENGE